AF483257

TRUSTING THE SELF WITHIN

TECHNIQUES FOR CONFIDENCE AND PEACE

DR. MINAKSHI BANSAL

Made with ♥ on the Notion Press Platform
www.notionpress.com

DEDICATION

This book is dedicated to all those who have ever doubted themselves, to those who are seeking a quieter place within amidst the noise of everyday life, and to those who have bravely shared their stories with me, teaching me the true meaning of resilience and grace. May this book serve as a beacon on your journey to finding and trusting your own inner strength.

Contents

Contents

Prayer

"Om Bhadram Karnebhih Shrinuyama Devah
Bhadram Pashyemakshabhiryajatrah
Sthirairangais Tushtuvamsastanubhih
Vyashema Devahitam Yadayuh
Svasti Na Indro Vriddhashravah
Svasti Nah Pusha Vishwavedah
Svasti Nastarkshyo Arishtanemih
Svasti No Brihaspatir Dadhatu
Om Shantih Shantih Shantih"

This mantra is a prayer for universal well-being, invoking the blessings of various deities for protection, health, and happiness. It emphasizes the importance of experiencing the auspicious through all senses and living a life aligned with divine purpose. The repetition of "Shantih" at the end signifies a deep desire for peace in the individual, the environment, and the universe at large. This mantra is often recited as a prayer for peace, prosperity, and the physical and spiritual well-being of all beings.

About The Author

Dr. Minakshi Bansal, born in the bustling metropolis of Delhi, India, has led a life steeped in artistry, scholarly pursuit, and an unwavering commitment to societal betterment. Following her marriage, she relocated to Ahmedabad, Gujarat, where she has since blossomed into a multifaceted beacon of inspiration for many. Dr. Minakshi is not only recognized as a gifted artist in the realm of Fine Arts but also as an esteemed author, a devoted social worker and a dedicated research scholar in Psychology. Her journey, marked by a profound dedication to elevating those around her, especially the downtrodden and underprivileged children of society, is a testament to her deep-seated belief in the transformative power of engagement and empathy.

From her earliest days, Minakshi was distinguished by an insatiable appetite for reading. Her literary universe was inhabited by characters and narratives that spanned ethical tales, motivational and inspirational stories, and the mythic parables imbued with life lessons. This voracious reading habit was not merely for personal edification but was driven by a desire to distill and disseminate the essence of these narratives to foster the development of students and peers alike. She was particularly captivated by the lives and teachings of historical figures and spiritual leaders such as Adi Shankaracharya, Swami Vivekananda, Dr. APJ Abdul Kalam, Mahamana Pandit Madan Mohan Malviya, Mahatma Gandhi, Sardar Vallabhai Patel, and Vinoba Bhave, among others. Their philosophies and life stories fueled her ambition to embody their ideals of resilience, selflessness, and relentless pursuit of knowledge.

Dr. Minakshi's academic and practical engagement with psychology has been equally noteworthy. As a research scholar, her focus has been on exploring the intricate tapestry of the human psyche, aiming to unlock the potential for psychological well-being and societal harmony. Her scholarly work is complemented by her active involvement in social work, where she employs her academic insights to make tangible differences in the lives of the underprivileged. Her endeavours in social work are characterized by an innovative approach that combines traditional wisdom with contemporary psychological practices to address the multifaceted challenges faced by these communities.

Her artistic talents, another facet of her diverse capabilities, are not merely a personal passion but also serve as a medium through which she communicates and connects with others. Her art, rich in symbolism and emotional depth, reflects her philosophical inquiries and social concerns, offering viewers a glimpse into the breadth of her intellect and the depth of her compassion.

In addition to her contributions to the arts and social sciences, Dr. Minakshi has embraced the healing arts of Pranic Healing, mastering the techniques developed by Master Choa Kok Sui. This practice, which focuses on the manipulation of Prana or life energy to heal the body and aura, has been both a personal journey of discovery and a means through which she extends her healing touch to others. Her proficiency in Pranic Healing is complemented by her advocacy and teaching of various forms of meditation aimed at rejuvenation, personal betterment, and the cultivation of harmony within individuals and communities alike.

Dr. Minakshi's life is a narrative of relentless pursuit, not just of personal achievement but of the upliftment and empowerment of society at large. Her diverse interests and talents—spanning the arts, literature, psychology, and the healing practices—converge on a singular path of service. She embodies the spirit of the luminaries who inspired her, channelling their legacy through her actions and teachings. Through her books, art, and social initiatives, she continues to inspire a new generation to embark on their own journeys of self-discovery, resilience, and altruism.

Her commitment to social betterment, particularly her focus on uplifting underprivileged children, reflects a deep understanding of the transformative potential of education and personal development. By integrating her knowledge of psychology, her artistic sensibilities, and her healing practices, Dr. Bansal has developed a holistic approach to social work that addresses both the immediate needs and the long-term well-being of the communities she serves.

As an author, Dr. Minakshi's writings offer a blend of inspirational insights, practical wisdom, and reflective contemplations drawn from her extensive reading and life experiences. Her books serve as a guide for those seeking to navigate the complexities of life with grace, resilience, and purpose. Through her narratives, she extends an invitation to her readers to explore the depths of their own potential and to contribute meaningfully to the collective well-being of society.

In Dr. Minakshi Bansal, we find a remarkable synthesis of the artist, the scholar, the healer, and the social activist. Her life's work stands as a beacon of hope and a source of inspiration for individuals seeking to make a difference in the world. Her story is a compelling reminder of the power of individual action, rooted in compassion and driven by a profound commitment to the betterment of humanity. Dr. Minakshi's legacy is not just in the tangible outcomes of her efforts but in the enduring spirit of inquiry, empathy, and service that she embodies.

Preface

As I sat down to write this book, I was driven by a simple, yet profound realization that had shaped much of my own life: the journey toward genuine self-trust and inner peace is perhaps one of the most crucial undertakings for anyone seeking a life of fulfillment and calm. This realization did not come easily nor quickly; it was the product of years of experiences, reflections, and, most importantly, the interactions I've had with countless individuals who shared their personal stories of struggle and success with me. Each story added a layer of understanding and pushed me further towards a deeper comprehension of how fundamentally interconnected confidence and peace really are.

This book is born from a desire to encapsulate those insights and offer them as a guide to others on this path. It is for anyone who has ever felt overwhelmed by doubt, fear, or turmoil – which, I believe, includes all of us at one point or another. Here, I present not just theories but practical strategies that can be woven into the fabric of daily life to foster a resilient, confident, and peaceful self.

Writing this book has been a journey in itself. It required me to delve deeply into both personal and shared human experiences, examining the very essence of what it means to trust oneself. Throughout this process, I have been reminded time and again of the transformative power of self-trust and how it can elevate one's life from mere existence to something much greater and more meaningful. This exploration is grounded in the belief that building confidence and finding inner peace are not only possible but essential for a well-lived life.

Each chapter of this book tackles different aspects of this belief, drawing from a broad spectrum of disciplines including psychology, philosophy, and personal development. My aim has been to provide a holistic view that addresses the varied dimensions of human experience – emotional, intellectual, and spiritual. The techniques and insights shared here are those that I have found to be most effective in not only my own life but also in the lives of those I have had the privilege to assist as a coach and mentor.

In writing this book, my hope is that it will serve as a gentle companion to those seeking to understand and harness their inner strengths. Whether you are someone struggling with self-doubt, a professional aiming to build greater confidence in your abilities, or simply someone who wishes to lead a more peaceful life, the contents herein are designed to assist you on your journey.

The structure of the book follows a natural progression, starting with understanding the nature of self-trust, exploring the impact of internal and external influences on our confidence, and finally, offering methods to cultivate and sustain inner peace. It's structured to be accessible, allowing readers to either progress from start to finish or to dive into specific sections as they feel drawn.

Importantly, while the advice and strategies are based on evidence and professional practice, they are meant to be adapted to fit individual needs and circumstances. I encourage you, the reader, to approach this book not as a manual that must be followed to the letter, but as a source of suggestions that you can select from and modify to suit your unique path toward self-trust and peace.

As you turn these pages, I invite you to engage actively with the content, reflect on your own experiences, and even challenge the ideas presented if they provoke thought or skepticism. It is through such active engagement that true learning and personal development occur. I also encourage you to practice the exercises and reflect on the insights shared, as understanding can only be deepened through action.

My deepest wish is that this book inspires you to embark on your own journey of self-discovery and growth. May it bring you closer to the confidence and peace you seek, and may you discover that the strength you need to achieve these states has been within you all along. Thank you for allowing me to be a part of your journey.

ONE

Embracing Vulnerability: The First Step to Self-Trust

Trusting oneself begins with the courageous act of embracing vulnerability. Vulnerability, often perceived as a weakness, is in fact a profound strength that forms the foundation of self-trust. When we allow ourselves to be vulnerable, we open up to the possibility of true connection with our inner selves and, by extension, with others.

Vulnerability starts with acknowledging one's feelings, fears, and desires without judgment. It requires an honest look at one's limitations and the acceptance of not always being in control. This might seem daunting because it goes against the grain of societal expectations that often equate vulnerability with inadequacy. However, embracing this aspect of our humanity is essential for growth. It is in the moments when we are most vulnerable that we are also the most open to learning and transformation.

Understanding the link between vulnerability and self-trust is crucial. Self-trust is not about never feeling doubts or fears; rather, it's about knowing that you can endure and grow from these experiences. Trusting oneself means believing in one's ability to manage the outcomes of one's decisions, no matter how uncertain. It involves stepping into the unknown and having faith in one's capacity to navigate it.

Building a Relationship with Uncertainty

A key part of embracing vulnerability is building a relationship with uncertainty. Life is inherently unpredictable, and learning to coexist with this unpredictability is a vital aspect of developing self-trust. It means making peace with not knowing everything and being comfortable with the idea that not all variables are within our control. This can start with small steps, like changing daily routines or making decisions without seeking absolute certainty about the outcomes.

Moreover, embracing uncertainty teaches resilience. It prepares us to handle life's inevitable ups and downs more effectively. Each challenge faced and navigated through boosts our confidence and reinforces our trust in our own abilities. Over time, this cultivated resilience builds a strong foundation of self-trust that can support us in all areas of life.

Cultivating Self-Compassion

Another important aspect of embracing vulnerability is cultivating self-compassion. Being hard on oneself is a common barrier to self-trust. When we meet our vulnerabilities with criticism rather than compassion, we erode our confidence and trust in ourselves. Self-compassion involves treating oneself with the same kindness, concern, and support one would show to a good friend.

Practicing self-compassion can start with simply noticing when we are being self-critical and consciously choosing to soften our internal dialogue. It's about recognizing that making mistakes and experiencing failures are part of being human. Each experience provides valuable lessons that contribute to our growth and understanding of ourselves.

Authenticity as a Pathway to Trust

Embracing vulnerability also paves the way for living authentically, which is integral to building self-trust. Authenticity means aligning one's actions with one's values and beliefs, rather than performing to meet external expectations. It involves expressing one's true self and not hiding one's feelings to fit into a mold. This congruence between thought, feeling, and action reinforces self-trust, because when we know we are being true to ourselves, we strengthen our trust in our own judgments and responses.

Living authentically requires courage and, often, a deliberate move away from societal norms or expectations. It can feel risky or uncomfortable, but the reward is a more satisfying and meaningful life. When we stop letting fear dictate our actions, we gain a profound sense of freedom and self-empowerment.

As we learn to embrace our vulnerability, we not only foster self-trust but also build deeper, more genuine connections with others. Vulnerability allows us to express our needs and boundaries more clearly, which enhances our relationships. It invites openness and intimacy, enabling others to see and connect with our true selves.

Embracing vulnerability is not a one-time event but a continuous process of growth and understanding. It involves regular self-reflection, a willingness to face our fears, and the courage to step outside our comfort zones. By doing so, we lay the groundwork for a resilient, confident, and peaceful life, firmly rooted in a deep trust in ourselves. Embracing vulnerability might be challenging, but it is one of the most rewarding paths to personal development and lasting self-trust.

"Embracing vulnerability is the first step toward inner strength; it's through our openness that we invite true connection and deep understanding into our lives. Vulnerability is not weakness; it's the courageous path to authentic self-discovery."

♡♡♡

TWO

UNDERSTANDING ANXIETY: ORIGINS AND OVERCOMING

Anxiety is a fundamental human experience, serving as a natural response to perceived threats and uncertainties. To manage and overcome anxiety effectively, it is crucial to understand its origins, manifestations, and the strategies that can mitigate its impact on our lives. This comprehension not only helps in alleviating immediate symptoms but also addresses the underlying triggers of anxiety, fostering a more resilient and peaceful existence.

The Roots of Anxiety

Anxiety often originates from a combination of biological, psychological, and environmental factors. From a biological standpoint, anxiety can be linked to genetics and brain chemistry, suggesting that some individuals are naturally predisposed to experiencing higher levels of anxiety. Psychological aspects, including one's upbringing, past traumas, and learned behaviors, also play significant roles. Environmentally, stressful life conditions such as financial instability, relationship problems, or intense work environments can trigger and exacerbate anxiety symptoms.

Recognizing the multifaceted nature of anxiety is the first step towards managing it. This recognition helps in identifying the specific sources and triggers in an individual's life, which is essential for effective intervention. It also cultivates a deeper empathy towards oneself and others dealing with anxiety, acknowledging that the condition is not a simple matter of being overly worried but a complex interplay of various factors.

The Physiology of Anxiety

Understanding the physiological response to anxiety is key to demystifying its overwhelming power. The body's fight-or-flight response, which is triggered during periods of anxiety, involves a series of hormonal changes and physiological reactions that prepare the body to either confront or flee from a threat. This response can be incredibly beneficial in genuinely dangerous situations, but when repeatedly triggered by everyday stressors, it can lead to chronic anxiety that is detrimental to overall health.

Symptoms of anxiety can vary widely but typically include racing thoughts, increased heart rate, rapid breathing, sweating, and feelings of dread or panic. By recognizing these symptoms as natural physiological responses, individuals can begin to implement strategies that help regulate their body's reactions and reduce the intensity of their anxiety.

Strategies for Overcoming Anxiety

Effective management of anxiety involves both immediate techniques to alleviate symptoms and long-term strategies to address underlying causes. Mindfulness and breathing exercises are powerful tools for immediate relief. These practices help shift focus from anxious thoughts to the present moment and slow down the body's fight-or-flight response, providing a sense of calm and control.

Cognitive-behavioral therapy (CBT) is another highly effective approach for treating anxiety. CBT works by helping individuals identify and challenge the negative thought patterns that fuel anxiety, replacing them with more realistic and positive perspectives. This therapy also involves gradually exposing the individual to anxiety-inducing situations in a controlled manner, which helps decrease sensitivity to these triggers over time.

Lifestyle Modifications

In addition to psychological interventions, lifestyle changes can significantly impact anxiety levels. Regular physical activity, a balanced diet, sufficient sleep, and avoiding substances like caffeine and alcohol that can exacerbate anxiety symptoms are crucial. Additionally, engaging in regular social activities and maintaining a supportive network of friends and family can provide emotional comfort and reduce feelings of isolation, which often accompany anxiety.

Another important aspect of overcoming anxiety involves creating a personal toolkit of resources and techniques tailored to individual needs. This might include activities like yoga, meditation, journaling, or artistic hobbies that encourage expression and self-reflection. Developing and regularly updating this toolkit can empower individuals to take active steps in managing their anxiety.

Understanding and overcoming anxiety is a dynamic process that requires a combination of self-awareness, therapeutic strategies, and lifestyle adjustments. By delving into the origins of anxiety and employing a comprehensive approach to treatment, individuals can reclaim their sense of calm and control. Overcoming anxiety is not about eliminating it entirely but learning to manage it effectively so that it no longer controls one's life. This journey, while challenging, is incredibly rewarding, as it leads to greater resilience, self-trust, and overall well-being.

"Anxiety often masks itself as a giant in our minds, but with the right techniques, we can shrink it down to a manageable size. Understand it, confront it, and watch it lose its power over you. Peace comes when we choose to face our fears, not when we wait for them to disappear."

♡♡♡

THREE

The Power of Positive Self-Talk

Positive self-talk is a transformative tool for enhancing self-esteem and overall mental health, acting as a catalyst for personal empowerment and self-fulfillment. This mental habit involves consciously generating affirmative thoughts about oneself and one's capabilities, countering the often automatic negative thoughts that can cloud our perceptions and judgments. Embracing positive self-talk can lead to significant improvements in our quality of life, influencing everything from our mood and stress levels to our relationships and career success.

Understanding Negative Thought Patterns

Before we can harness the power of positive self-talk, it is essential to understand the nature and impact of negative thought patterns. These are the automatic, often critical and pessimistic thoughts that typically arise in response to challenging situations. Common examples include thoughts like "I can't do this," "I'm not good enough," or "Everything is going wrong." Such thoughts not only dampen morale but can also become self-fulfilling prophecies, leading to decreased motivation and adverse outcomes.

The origin of these negative thoughts often lies in past experiences, societal pressures, or internalized expectations from family or cultural norms. They are reinforced by repetition and acceptance as truth. Breaking this cycle requires recognizing these patterns as merely thoughts, not facts, and consciously choosing to respond with positive affirmations.

Cultivating a Practice of Positive Self-Talk

To cultivate a practice of positive self-talk, start by observing your internal dialogue, especially during times of stress or disappointment. Identify the negative thoughts and challenge their validity. Replace them with positive affirmations that are not only optimistic but also realistic. This might mean shifting from "I always mess up" to "I can learn from my mistakes and improve."

Implementing this practice involves several steps:

Awareness: Become aware of the moments when negative thoughts arise.

Pause and assess: Stop to consider whether these thoughts are helpful or hindering.

Reframe: Consciously choose to reframe the thought in a positive or constructive light.

This reframing can be strengthened through various techniques such as journaling, where you can write down negative thoughts and transform them into positive statements. Another effective method is using positive affirmations daily, which can help reset the mental narrative from pessimism to optimism.

The Role of Positive Self-Talk in Stress Reduction and Resilience Building

Positive self-talk plays a crucial role in stress reduction by altering how we perceive and react to stressors. Instead of viewing a stressful situation as threatening or insurmountable, positive self-talk encourages us to see it as a challenge that can be managed or overcome. This shift in perspective reduces the physiological and psychological impacts of stress, such as anxiety and tension, and promotes a more balanced emotional state.

Furthermore, positive self-talk contributes to building resilience by fostering a mindset that is more adaptable to adversity. Resilient individuals are characterized by their ability to maintain a positive outlook and bounce back from setbacks. By consistently engaging in positive self-talk, individuals can cultivate these resilient qualities, enhancing their ability to navigate through difficulties with greater ease and confidence.

Positive Self-Talk as a Tool for Achieving Goals

Adopting a habit of positive self-talk can also significantly impact one's ability to achieve personal and professional goals. By maintaining a mindset that focuses on one's strengths and potential, positive self-talk boosts self-confidence and motivation. It acts as a mental support system, especially when facing challenges or pursuing long-term objectives. This supportive inner voice reminds us of our capabilities and encourages persistence, which is crucial for overcoming obstacles and reaching success.

Moreover, positive self-talk enhances problem-solving skills by keeping the mind open to creative solutions and new opportunities. Instead of getting overwhelmed by problems, a positively oriented mind explores possible actions and stays focused on progress, not perfection.

The power of positive self-talk is immense and multifaceted. It transforms not only our self-perception and emotional health but also our interactions with the world around us. By making a commitment to replace negative thoughts with positive ones, we can foster a more fulfilling and empowered life. As we practice and strengthen this skill, the benefits extend beyond the individual, influencing our relationships, professional success, and overall well-being. Embracing positive self-talk is not merely about being optimistic but about creating a sustainable foundation for a resilient and joyful life.

"Positive self-talk is the script you write for the life you want to lead. Speak to yourself with compassion and encouragement, and the external world will reflect this kindness. Every word we tell ourselves plants a seed for our future selves."

♡♡♡

FOUR

MINDFULNESS: LIVING IN THE PRESENT MOMENT

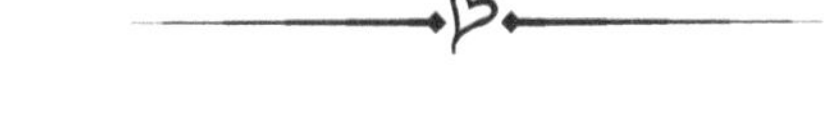

Mindfulness is a powerful practice that involves maintaining a moment-by-moment awareness of our thoughts, feelings, bodily sensations, and surrounding environment. It encourages a state of active, open attention to the present, which allows individuals to observe their thoughts and feelings without judgment. This practice is rooted in Buddhist meditation but has been adapted in various forms across different cultures and is widely recognized in the modern psychological context for its benefits in reducing stress, enhancing emotional regulation, and increasing overall mental clarity.

The Essence of Mindfulness

The core of mindfulness lies in its simplicity and accessibility. It is the art of being fully engaged with whatever we are doing at the moment, free from distraction or judgment. This can be as mundane as feeling the sensation of air entering and leaving the nostrils during breathing or as complex as fully engaging in a conversation without planning what to say next. By focusing our attention on the present, mindfulness counteracts one of the mind's default modes characterized by an autopilot state where we are mechanically performing tasks without true awareness.

Cultivating Mindfulness Through Meditation

One of the most effective ways to cultivate mindfulness is through meditation. Mindfulness meditation involves sitting quietly and paying attention to thoughts, sounds, the sensations of breathing, or parts of the body. The practice involves observing without criticism; if the mind begins to race, the practice is to bring attention back to the present without judgment.

Many mindfulness meditation techniques begin with the breath: focusing attentively on the inhalation and exhalation, noticing when the mind wanders, and gently redirecting the focus back to the breath. This practice can be done for just a few minutes a day but can significantly impact one's ability to stay centered and calm throughout daily activities.

Integrating Mindfulness into Daily Life

Beyond formal meditation, mindfulness can be integrated into daily life by cultivating a deliberate awareness of our actions, thoughts, and feelings. This can be as simple as paying attention to the sensations of your feet touching the ground as you walk, or how your body feels when sitting or standing. Even routine activities like washing dishes, eating, or driving can be opportunities for mindfulness practice.

Another practical application is the "mindful pause"—taking short breaks throughout the day to simply breathe and be present. These pauses are especially beneficial in high-stress environments or during busy workdays, helping to reset and refocus the mind.

Mindfulness and Emotional Regulation

Mindfulness significantly impacts emotional regulation by changing how we experience emotions. By practicing mindfulness, individuals learn to observe their emotions without being overwhelmed by them. This observational distance allows one to recognize and accept feelings without rushing to react or judge. Such a perspective gives room to choose how to respond to emotions, which is particularly useful in managing anger, anxiety, or sadness.

Mindfulness in Relationships

Mindfulness also plays a crucial role in enhancing relationships. By being fully present with others, we can engage more deeply and respond more thoughtfully. Mindful listening, for instance, involves giving full attention to what the other person is saying without planning the next thing to say or judging what they are saying. This fosters better communication and more meaningful connections.

Mindfulness and Physical Health

In addition to its mental and emotional benefits, mindfulness has positive implications for physical health. Research has shown that regular mindfulness practice can reduce stress, lower blood pressure, improve sleep, and alleviate gastrointestinal difficulties. Furthermore, mindfulness has been linked to enhanced immune response and faster recovery from illness.

Mindfulness is a profound practice that offers numerous benefits across various aspects of life. It involves more than just meditation; it is about cultivating a greater awareness of the richness of each moment. By living more mindfully, we not only enhance our own well-being but also contribute to the well-being of those around us. Whether through dedicated meditation practices or integrating mindful moments throughout the day, the practice of mindfulness is a valuable tool for anyone seeking to lead a more conscious, connected, and fulfilling life.

"Mindfulness isn't just a practice; it's a way of living. By staying present, we anchor ourselves against the tides of uncertainty and stress. Find peace in the moment, and the chaos of the world becomes manageable."

FIVE

Decoding Stress: Strategies to Reduce Its Impact

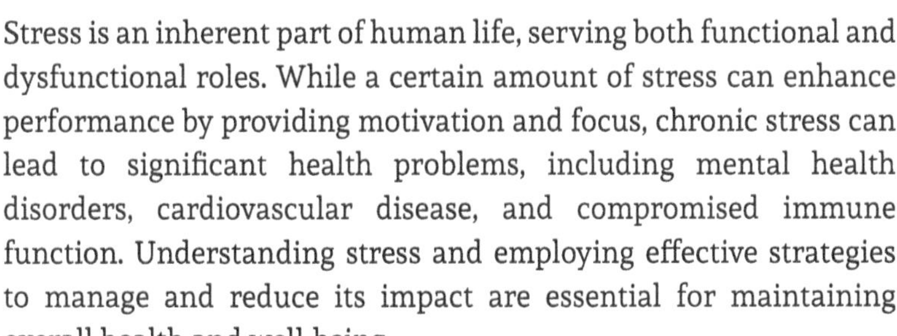

Stress is an inherent part of human life, serving both functional and dysfunctional roles. While a certain amount of stress can enhance performance by providing motivation and focus, chronic stress can lead to significant health problems, including mental health disorders, cardiovascular disease, and compromised immune function. Understanding stress and employing effective strategies to manage and reduce its impact are essential for maintaining overall health and well-being.

Understanding the Nature of Stress

Stress is the body's natural response to any demand or threat. When you sense danger—whether it's real or imagined—the body's defenses kick into high gear in a rapid, automatic process known as the "fight-or-flight" reaction. The stress response is the body's way of protecting you. When working properly, it helps you stay focused, energetic, and alert. In emergency situations, stress can save your life by giving you extra strength to defend yourself or spurring you to slam on the brakes to avoid an accident.

However, beyond a certain point, stress stops being helpful and starts causing major damage to your health, mood, productivity, relationships, and quality of life. It is crucial to understand that stress is not an external event itself, but rather your body's response to perceived threats or demands.

Identifying Sources of Stress

The first step in managing stress is to identify its sources. These can vary widely and may not always be obvious. Stressors can include major life changes, work difficulties, relationship problems, financial problems, and everyday hassles. Keeping a stress journal can help identify regular, recurring stressors and the way you deal with them. Each time you feel stressed, keep track of it in your journal. As you keep a daily log, you will begin to see patterns and common themes.

Techniques to Reduce Stress

Once the sources of stress are identified, the next step is to implement strategies to deal with them. There are numerous techniques to reduce stress, each suited to different situations and personal preferences.

Mindfulness and Meditation: These practices help center the mind and reduce overthinking, which can exacerbate stress. Techniques such as guided imagery, deep breathing exercises, and mindfulness meditation can reduce the immediate feelings of stress by calming the mind and body, providing a break from stressors.

Physical Activity: Exercise is one of the most important things you can do to combat stress. It might seem contradictory, but physical stress through exercise can relieve mental stress. The benefits are strongest when you exercise regularly. People who exercise regularly are less likely to experience anxiety than those who don't exercise.

Improved Time Management: Often, stress arises from feeling like you don't have enough time to get everything done. By improving time management skills, such as prioritizing tasks, setting boundaries, and taking breaks, you can reduce stress levels by making your day more manageable.

Developing Healthy Relationships: Strong, supportive relationships are a buffer against stress. Spend time with family and friends who help you relax and make you laugh. Being part of a friend network gives you a sense of belonging and self-worth, which can help in tough times.

Professional Help: When stress becomes chronic and overwhelming, professional help might be necessary. Therapists can assist in developing specific strategies to manage stress effectively and improve mental health.

Creating a Stress-Resilient Lifestyle

In addition to specific techniques, creating a lifestyle that helps prevent stress is crucial. This involves regular physical activity, maintaining a healthy diet, getting enough sleep, and engaging in leisure activities. Moreover, developing resilience, the ability to cope with stress and rise above adversity, is critical. This can be fostered through positive thinking, flexibility, problem-solving skills, and the ability to manage emotions.

Adopting a Positive Outlook

Transforming how you think about stress can also impact its effects on your health. Studies have shown that if you perceive stress as a challenge rather than a threat, you can reduce the wear and tear on your body and mind. Adopting a more positive outlook and learning to think more optimistically can also enhance your ability to manage stress.

While stress is an unavoidable aspect of life, it can be managed and controlled with the right techniques and lifestyle choices. By understanding the sources and mechanics of stress and actively employing strategies to counteract its effects, individuals can maintain their health and enhance their quality of life. These efforts not only improve personal well-being but also enrich the lives of those around us.

"Stress, when understood and managed, can become a tool rather than a tormentor. Recognize its signals, learn its patterns, and teach yourself to dance gracefully with it. Only then can we turn our stress into a stepping stone rather than a stumbling block."

SIX

Building Resilience: Lessons in Recovery and Strength

Resilience is the remarkable ability of individuals to bounce back from setbacks, adapt well to change, and keep going in the face of adversity. Developing resilience is not merely about returning to the original state before difficulty struck, but rather growing and potentially becoming stronger through the process of overcoming challenges. This capability does not arise in a vacuum; it is cultivated through experiences, personal outlook, and deliberate practice.

Understanding the Foundations of Resilience

At its core, resilience involves positive adaptation within the context of significant adversity. This concept is not a trait that people either have or do not have. It involves behaviors, thoughts, and actions that can be learned and developed by anyone. Key components of resilience include a positive attitude, optimism, the ability to regulate emotions, and the ability to see failure as a form of helpful feedback.

Learning from past experiences and seeing them as an opportunity to learn and grow is essential for developing resilience. People who are resilient tend to maintain a positive outlook and view life's challenges as opportunities to improve, rather than insurmountable obstacles.

Factors Contributing to Resilience

Several factors contribute to resilience, which can be categorized broadly into personal qualities and external support systems.

Personal Qualities: These include self-awareness, independence, the ability to manage strong feelings and impulses, and good problem-solving skills. Self-awareness is crucial as it helps one understand what is causing stress and how to deal with it effectively. Independence strengthens the resolve to navigate challenges without undue reliance on others. Moreover, effective emotion regulation and problem-solving skills enable individuals to look at problems from various angles and find solutions that may not be immediately apparent.

External Support Systems: These are equally important and include relationships with friends and family that provide love and trust, offer encouragement, and accept without judgment. Community support, including networks of friends and community groups, also plays a critical role in fostering resilience by providing emotional and practical support.

Strategies to Build and Strengthen Resilience

Building resilience is a personal journey that involves developing both internal coping skills and cultivating external resources. Here are several effective strategies:

Maintain Connections: Prioritize building strong, positive relationships with family and friends who can offer support and acceptance in times of need. Being part of a community or support group can also provide a buffer against feelings of loneliness and isolation.

Foster Wellness: Self-care is crucial for resilience. Taking care of your mind and body enhances your ability to cope with situations that require resilience. Practice mindfulness, maintain regular physical activity, get adequate sleep, eat healthily, and engage in leisure activities.

Embrace Healthy Thoughts: Keep things in perspective, accept that change is a part of living, and replace negative thoughts with more balanced and constructive ones. Viewing stressful situations from a broader perspective helps reduce the fear and isolation that can accompany adversity.

Seek Solutions: Actively engage in problem-solving. Identify what can be done to alleviate or manage the problem, and take decisive steps to confront challenges directly. This proactive approach fosters a sense of control and personal efficacy, which are vital components of resilience.

Learn from Experiences: Reflect on past experiences that have involved adversity and recall how you've successfully navigated them. This reflection enhances your confidence in dealing with current and future challenges and provides a reminder that past troubles have been resolved and can be managed.

Set Realistic Goals: Develop realistic and achievable goals to build confidence and a sense of achievement. Even small accomplishments can help you move towards the changes you desire and fortify your resilience.

Resilience is not a quality that appears magically within us; it's something that needs to be cultivated actively. Through understanding its foundations, strengthening personal qualities, leveraging support systems, and employing practical strategies, individuals can enhance their capacity to recover from setbacks. By fostering resilience, not only can one navigate life's inevitable challenges more effectively, but also thrive and grow in the face of adversity. The journey of building resilience is a profound process of personal development, offering lessons in recovery and strength that can last a lifetime.

"Resilience is the quiet power that propels us forward through adversity. It's built through battles won, lost, and those we chose to walk away from. Each experience, no matter how small, fortifies our spirit for the challenges ahead."

♡♡♡

SEVEN

Harnessing the Power of Visualization

Visualization is a powerful mental technique that involves using one's imagination to envision specific behaviors or events occurring in one's life. Often used by athletes to enhance their performance, visualization is a practice that can benefit virtually anyone in achieving their goals and improving their reality. By creating detailed mental images of desired outcomes, individuals can foster a deeper connection between their mind and body, making it easier to manifest these visions into reality.

Understanding Visualization

Visualization, or mental imagery, is more than simple daydreaming. It involves consciously using one's imagination to create vivid and detailed images of behaviors or events that one wishes to manifest or accomplish. This practice engages the brain in a way that mimics actual participation in the visualized activity. Neurons in our brains, those electrically excitable cells that transmit information, interpret imagery as equivalent to a real-life action. This causes the brain to encode this visualization as a real memory, providing both physical and psychological benefits such as enhanced motivation, increased confidence, and improved motor performance.

The Science Behind Visualization

Research in the field of sports psychology and neurology has shown that visualization can enhance physical performance and increase the likelihood of achieving one's goals. This is achieved by programming the brain for success. Visualization impacts the brain's motor cortex, which is responsible for coordinating body movements. Studies have demonstrated that even without physical activity, visualizing the performance of a sport can enhance muscle strength.

The process also stimulates the same neural pathways in the brain as when performing the task physically. For example, a basketball player who visualizes making free throws activates similar brain areas involved when actually shooting the ball. This mental rehearsal primes the body for physical execution, enhancing muscle memory and overall performance.

Techniques for Effective Visualization

For visualization to be effective, it must be practiced regularly and with clear intent. Here are some key techniques to enhance the practice:

Create a Detailed Image: The more detailed your visualization, the more effective it will be. Include as many senses as you can—sight, sound, touch, even smell and taste. If you're visualizing running a race, for example, imagine the sound of the crowd, the feeling of your feet hitting the track, the adrenaline pumping through your veins.

Incorporate Emotion: Emotionally charged visualizations are more likely to impact behavior and outcomes. Engage your emotions by feeling the joy, pride, or satisfaction that would accompany achieving your goal.

Practice Consistently: Like any skill, visualization gets better with practice. Set aside a few minutes each day to engage in mental imagery. Consistency is key to making visualization a productive part of your success strategy.

Use Guided Imagery: For those who find it difficult to practice visualization on their own, guided imagery resources are available. These can be guided meditation recordings or working with a coach who can lead you through the imagery.

Combine with Real Efforts: While visualization is powerful, it must be combined with actual efforts towards the goal. Visualization should be used as a complement to physical practice and other real-world preparation.

Applications Beyond Sports

While athletes may use visualization most prominently, this technique is not limited to sports. It can be equally effective in public speaking, performing arts, interviews, and even daily interactions. For instance, visualizing a successful presentation can help reduce anxiety and improve performance when the actual moment arrives. Similarly, one can use visualization to prepare for challenging conversations, envisioning oneself handling the situation with confidence and calm.

Visualization and Goal Setting

Visualization also plays a crucial role in goal setting. By visualizing the end goal, individuals can maintain focus and stay motivated. It serves as a mental rehearsal, preparing the mind and body for the actions required to achieve these goals. When goals are visualized vividly and frequently, they become ingrained in the subconscious, making them seem more attainable and real, which in turn boosts commitment and perseverance.

Visualization is a potent tool in the arsenal for personal and professional development. By harnessing the power of the mind to envision success, individuals can improve their chances of achieving their goals and enhancing their performance in various aspects of life. Regular practice of this technique can transform visualization from mere mental imagery into a trigger for actual success and fulfillment. As with any skill, the benefits of visualization are most pronounced when it is applied consistently and in alignment with one's actions and goals. This mental strategy is not just about seeing the outcome but also about setting the stage for real-world achievements.

"Visualization is not about dreaming; it's about creating a vision for your life that compels you to act. See the future you desire, then lay the foundations in the present. What the mind can conceive, it can achieve."

♡♡♡

EIGHT
CULTIVATING EMOTIONAL INTELLIGENCE

Emotional intelligence (EI) is the ability to understand and manage one's own emotions, as well as recognize and influence the emotions of others. It is a critical skill that impacts various aspects of life, including interpersonal relationships, workplace dynamics, and personal well-being. Cultivating emotional intelligence can lead to more effective communication, better problem-solving skills, and improved conflict resolution abilities.

Understanding Emotional Intelligence

The concept of emotional intelligence encompasses several key skills: self-awareness, self-regulation, motivation, empathy, and social skills.

Self-awareness involves recognizing one's own emotions and how they affect thoughts and behavior.

Self-regulation refers to the ability to control or redirect disruptive emotions and impulses and adapt to changing circumstances.

Motivation includes a passion to work for reasons that go beyond money or status and a propensity to pursue goals with energy and persistence.

Empathy is the ability to understand the emotional makeup of other people.

Social skills refer to managing relationships to move people in the desired direction, whether in leading, negotiating, or working as part of a team.

By developing these areas, individuals can enhance their emotional intelligence, leading to more positive outcomes both personally and professionally.

Developing Self-Awareness

The first step in cultivating emotional intelligence is increasing self-awareness. This involves understanding your emotions and their impact on your behavior and decisions. Regular reflection on your emotional responses to different situations can help in identifying patterns and triggers in your emotional landscape. Techniques such as journaling, meditation, and mindfulness can facilitate this self-exploration, providing deeper insights into personal emotional states and how these affect interactions with others.

Improving Self-Regulation

Once self-awareness is established, the next step is to work on self-regulation. This involves learning how to manage your responses to emotions so that they are appropriate and do not disrupt personal or professional life. Techniques for improving self-regulation include:

Breathing exercises and relaxation techniques to reduce the intensity of emotional reactions.

Delaying response to allow time to think and assess the situation before acting.

Cognitive reappraisal to change the emotional response by altering the interpretation of the situation.

Building these skills can help in maintaining control over one's emotions and behaving in a consistently professional and thoughtful manner.

Enhancing Motivation

Intrinsic motivation, a part of emotional intelligence, drives individuals to pursue their goals for personal satisfaction rather than external rewards. Enhancing motivation involves understanding and reconnecting with the reasons why you are committed to your goals. Setting clear, achievable goals and celebrating small achievements can keep motivation high. Additionally, aligning personal values with daily tasks can enhance the intrinsic motivation needed for sustained effort and resilience.

Building Empathy

Empathy is a critical skill within emotional intelligence that involves understanding and sharing the feelings of others. To develop empathy, practice active listening, which means fully concentrating on what is being said rather than just passively hearing the message. It involves acknowledging the other person's perspective and responding appropriately. Exercises such as role-playing or engaging with diverse groups can also enhance empathetic skills by exposing an individual to different perspectives and emotional experiences.

Strengthening Social Skills

Social skills in emotional intelligence involve the ability to manage relationships effectively, enabling people to move in a desired direction, whether toward agreement in negotiations, enthusiasm about a vision, or teamwork in collaborative efforts. Developing strong social skills requires:

Effective communication, which includes not only speaking clearly and assertively but also being able to listen intently and respond appropriately.

Conflict resolution skills, which involve identifying solutions that all parties can endorse, or at least accept.

Influencing skills, which are about affecting the views and actions of others in a positive way.

Integrating Emotional Intelligence into Everyday Life

Integrating emotional intelligence into everyday life means practicing these skills in real-time. It's about making a conscious effort to pause and choose how to act or respond in various situations. This might involve taking a few deep breaths when feeling overwhelmed, asking for feedback on how your actions affect others, or spending time reflecting on personal and professional interactions at the end of the day to evaluate and learn from them.

Cultivating emotional intelligence is a continual process that significantly enhances an individual's ability to engage with the world. It improves personal relationships, professional interactions, and overall psychological well-being. By systematically developing the components of emotional intelligence—self-awareness, self-regulation, motivation, empathy, and social skills—individuals can achieve a better understanding of themselves and others, leading to more fulfilling and successful lives.

"Emotional intelligence is the invisible skill that smooths rough edges in relationships and polishes our interactions. It teaches us to listen not just to respond, but to understand. Nurture it well, and watch your relationships flourish."

NINE

Setting Boundaries: The Art of Saying No

Setting boundaries is an essential skill for maintaining a healthy emotional and psychological state. It involves understanding your limits and knowing when you need to draw lines or say no to workloads, demands, or behaviors that cause undue stress or discomfort. Setting effective boundaries not only protects your self-esteem and sense of autonomy but also improves your relationships by promoting mutual respect.

Understanding the Importance of Boundaries

Boundaries are the limits and rules we set for ourselves within relationships. A person with healthy boundaries can say no when they want to, but they are also comfortable opening up to intimacy and close relationships. The key to effectively setting boundaries lies in understanding the value they bring to your life. They help control the physical and emotional space between yourself and others, making it possible to separate your own feelings, needs, and responsibilities from others'.

When boundaries are weak or nonexistent, you may overextend yourself because you are unable to say no, leading to stress, burnout, and even resentment towards others. Conversely, too rigid boundaries might lead to isolation, as you may withdraw too much from social interactions. Finding the right balance is crucial.

Recognizing When Boundaries Are Needed

You may need to set or reinforce boundaries when you feel discomfort, resentment, or annoyance—feelings that often indicate that others are pushing your limits or that your limits are too lax. Other signs include feeling excessively worried about how others will respond to your performance at work or feeling taken advantage of in personal or professional relationships.

Identifying the need for boundaries is the first step, followed by clearly understanding where adjustments are necessary. This could involve your emotional availability, your time, or your physical space.

How to Set Healthy Boundaries

Self-awareness: Begin by understanding what you can tolerate and accept and what makes you feel uncomfortable or stressed. These feelings help determine where limits need to be set.

Clear Communication: Once you know the boundaries you want to set, communicate them clearly, calmly, and consistently. Use "I" statements to express your needs without blaming the other person, such as "I need to have some time to myself when I get home from work before I am ready to talk."

Be Direct: Many fear that setting boundaries might hurt a relationship. However, understanding that healthy relationships depend on maintaining effective personal boundaries is crucial. Be direct but respectful in asserting your needs.

Give Yourself Permission to Set Boundaries: Remind yourself that having boundaries is a right and necessary for your mental health and well-being. You have a duty to protect and respect yourself.

Practice Saying No: Many people find it difficult to say no because they fear rejection or want to avoid hurting others. However, saying no is a vital skill for maintaining your boundaries. Practice in situations that are less challenging before addressing more significant boundary challenges.

Start Small: If setting boundaries feels overwhelming, start with a small, non-threatening boundary. Gradually, as you become more accustomed to asserting your needs, you can tackle more challenging boundary settings.

Handling Pushback on Boundaries

When you first start setting boundaries, you might face resistance. Others might be accustomed to your previous openness and availability. Here's how you can handle pushback:

Stay Firm and Reiterate: If someone pushes against a boundary, it's important to reassert it clearly and firmly. Repeat your statement or request. Don't back down, and don't feel compelled to provide an excessive explanation. Your needs are enough.

Manage Guilt and Anxiety: Setting boundaries can sometimes lead to guilt and anxiety, especially if you're not used to standing up for yourself. Remember that setting boundaries is not just beneficial for you, but for others as well, as it leads to healthier and more respectful relationships.

Seek Support: If you're struggling with setting boundaries, seek support from friends, a mentor, or a therapist who can help you strengthen your resolve and make you feel supported and less alone in your efforts.

Integrating Boundaries into Your Life

Regularly review the boundaries you've set. Consider what's working and what isn't. Are there boundaries that need adjustment? Are you continuing to respect your own limits? This ongoing process helps you maintain your boundaries and teaches others to respect them.

Setting boundaries is a fundamental aspect of developing and maintaining healthy relationships and a healthy psyche. It requires understanding your needs, clearly communicating your limits, and being willing to uphold these boundaries when they are challenged. With practice, setting boundaries becomes less daunting and more empowering, leading to increased self-esteem, reduced stress, and healthier interactions.

"Setting boundaries is the ultimate act of self-respect. It communicates to others that your feelings, time, and needs are important. When we set boundaries, we teach others how to treat us."

♡♡♡

TEN

Achieving Balance: Work, Life, and Inner Harmony

Achieving a balanced life is a pursuit that many find elusive. Balance in this context does not necessarily mean an equal division of hours between work and personal life, but rather finding a harmony that allows for satisfaction in both without feeling overburdened or overwhelmed by either. This harmony is crucial for maintaining physical, emotional, and mental health, and requires a strategic and mindful approach to how we allocate our time and energy.

Understanding the Importance of Balance

The concept of work-life balance is fundamentally about creating an environment where one can thrive both professionally and personally. An imbalance can lead to stress, burnout, and a host of other mental and physical health issues. Balance, therefore, is not a luxury but a critical component of sustainable success and health.

Effective work-life balance means having the flexibility to get things done in your professional life while having time and energy left to enjoy your personal life. It is about prioritizing different responsibilities and pleasures in a way that does not compromise your health or sense of well-being.

Identifying Signs of Imbalance

Recognizing the signs of imbalance is the first step towards creating a more harmonious life. Some common indicators include:

Constant fatigue - feeling tired almost all the time, irrespective of how much rest you get.

Persistent stress - feeling that the pressures of life are endless and insurmountable.

Health problems - experiencing frequent illness, headaches, or muscle tension.

Neglected relationships - not having enough time for family or friends.

Poor work performance - due to a lack of focus or motivation as a result of being stretched too thin.

Identifying these symptoms early can help you take corrective action before the situation worsens.

Strategies for Achieving Balance

Achieving balance requires intentional actions and sometimes significant changes in both mindset and lifestyle. Here are some strategies to help create a more balanced life:

Set clear priorities and boundaries: Decide what is most important to you and set your boundaries accordingly. This might mean learning to say no at work or deciding not to check emails during family meals. Being clear about your priorities helps you make decisions that align with your goals for both work and personal fulfillment.

Leverage flexibility: If your job allows for flexible hours or telecommuting, take advantage of these options. Flexibility can reduce stress and increase productivity by allowing you to work at times when you are most efficient.

Manage your time effectively: Use tools and techniques that enhance productivity, such as task lists, calendars, and apps designed to minimize distractions and automate tasks. Effective time management can free up more time to be spent on personal interests or relaxation.

Cultivate efficiency at work: Strive to be efficient while at work to maximize productivity. This could involve delegating tasks, improving your working conditions, or continuously enhancing your skills to perform better.

Ensure regular self-care: Self-care should be a priority, not a luxury. This includes adequate sleep, nutrition, exercise, and downtime. Engaging regularly in activities that you enjoy and that relax you can replenish your energy and focus.

Maintain robust social connections: Spend quality time with family and friends. Social relationships are crucial for emotional well-being and can provide a counterbalance to work-related stress.

Seek professional guidance: Sometimes, achieving balance can be challenging, especially when feeling overwhelmed. Professional advice from a career counselor, life coach, or therapist might be necessary to help reassess priorities and learn coping strategies.

Integration into Everyday Life

Integrating balance into your daily life requires consistent effort. Reflect regularly on your lifestyle and adjust as needed. Life changes, and so too might your ideas about what balance means. Regularly check in with yourself about your current state of harmony and make adjustments as necessary.

Achieving balance between work, life, and inner harmony is an ongoing process that demands attention and intention. It requires setting priorities, managing time well, and making conscious choices in favor of a fulfilling and healthy life. While challenges in maintaining balance are inevitable, the benefits of striving for it—a healthier, more satisfying, and productive life—are immense. Recognizing the importance of balance and actively working towards it can lead to lasting improvements in all areas of your life.

"Achieving work-life balance isn't about equal hours; it's about equal harmony. Prioritize your tasks, but never forget that taking care of yourself is the most productive thing you can do. Balance is not found, it's created."

ELEVEN

INTUITION AS A GUIDE: LEARNING TO LISTEN

Intuition is often described as a gut feeling, a sense, or a sixth sense that informs us without any logical reasoning. It is an instinctive knowing without conscious reasoning. Learning to listen to and trust this inner voice can be a powerful tool for making decisions and navigating complex situations. This guide will delve into what intuition is, how it works, and practical ways to develop and trust this often-overlooked cognitive skill.

Understanding Intuition

Intuition operates at the intersection of experience and subconscious knowledge. It pulls from vast amounts of observations and experiences that are stored in our subconscious, providing us with answers that might not be immediately obvious to our rational mind. Intuitive insights often come quickly, without detailed deliberation. They are the brain's way of rapidly drawing on stored memories, patterns, and knowledge to offer a solution or reaction.

The Science Behind Intuition

Modern psychology and neuroscience have started to recognize the value of intuition. Studies show that intuition is a key part of how our brains process information. The brain's limbic system, which is involved in feeling and reacting, does not rely on language or rational thought processes. This part of the brain processes information much faster than the conscious, rational mind, which is why intuitive insights can seem to come from "nowhere."

Differentiating Intuition from Impulse

It is crucial to differentiate between intuition and impulse. Impulse is a sudden, perhaps irrational urge to do something, often driven by emotion. Intuition, on the other hand, is a quick understanding that comes from a deep-seated knowledge and experience. Impulses are typically reactive and not always aligned with long-term goals or well-being, while intuition often aligns with a deeper part of ourselves and our core values.

Cultivating Intuitive Skills

Developing intuition is akin to honing any other skill; it requires practice, attention, and a conducive environment. Here are some steps to enhance your intuitive abilities:

Mindfulness and Meditation: Regular mindfulness and meditation help quiet the mind and reduce noise from constant thoughts and distractions. This mental quietness is essential for intuition to surface and be noticed.

Reflective Practices: Keeping a journal can help you track decisions where you followed your intuition and the outcomes of those decisions. Reflecting on these can help reinforce your trust in your intuitive insights.

Attuning to Your Body: Often, intuition is felt physically — a gut feeling, a heart pull, or a physical sensation of comfort or discomfort. Pay attention to these bodily signals as part of your decision-making process.

Spend Time in Nature: Nature has a calming effect on the mind and can help enhance your receptiveness to intuitive thoughts. The natural environment reduces the mental load that often suppresses intuition.

Ask for Intuitive Insights: When faced with a decision, consciously ask yourself for an intuitive response and wait for an internal answer. This can be as simple as asking, "What do I need to know?" and seeing what arises.

Trusting Your Intuition

Trusting your intuition is as important as developing it. This can be challenging, especially in a society that prizes rationality and concrete evidence over feelings and instincts. Here are ways to build trust in your intuition:

Start Small: Begin by trusting your intuition on small, low-risk decisions. This can build your confidence in relying on your gut for more significant decisions.

Acknowledge Your Successes: When an intuitive decision leads to a positive outcome, acknowledge it. This reinforcement helps build trust in your intuitive capabilities.

Balance Intuition with Rationality: While intuition can guide you, balancing it with rational thought can provide a comprehensive decision-making strategy. Use intuition to get insights, but also weigh these insights with rational analysis when necessary.

Integrating Intuition in Daily Life

Integrating intuition into daily life means actively making space for it in your decision-making processes. It involves slowing down, listening to your inner signals, and allowing yourself the quiet and space needed for these insights to emerge.

Intuition is a powerful cognitive process that supplements logical analysis and enhances decision-making. By understanding, developing, and trusting your intuition, you can tap into a deeper wisdom that can guide you in making more aligned and authentic choices. This balanced approach can lead to more fulfilling and effective personal and professional lives.

"Let your intuition lead you occasionally; it's the whisper of your deepest self, guiding you along your path. Trusting it can feel like a leap into the dark, but every step reveals more of the light. Listen closely, and you'll find clarity."

♡♡♡

TWELVE

THE ROLE OF PHYSICAL HEALTH IN MENTAL WELL-BEING

Physical health and mental well-being are deeply interconnected, with each significantly influencing the other. Good physical health can promote better mental and emotional well-being, while poor physical health can increase the risk of developing mental health problems. Understanding this relationship can help individuals prioritize both physical and mental health to enhance overall quality of life.

Understanding the Connection Between Physical and Mental Health

The connection between physical and mental health is bidirectional; not only can poor physical health lead to an increased risk of developing mental health problems, but poor mental health can also have a profound impact on physical health, potentially leading to an increased risk of some conditions.

Several physiological mechanisms underline the link between physical and mental health:

Neurochemical: Physical activity stimulates the release of endorphins, chemicals in the brain that act as natural painkillers and mood elevators. Regular physical activity also stimulates the release of neurotransmitters like serotonin and dopamine, which play an essential part in regulating mood.

Inflammatory Response: Chronic inflammation has been linked to a range of health issues, including mood disorders like depression and anxiety. Regular physical activity helps decrease inflammatory markers.

Stress Reduction: Exercise reduces levels of the body's stress hormones, such as adrenaline and cortisol. It also stimulates the production of endorphins, which are natural mood lifters.

Improved Sleep: Physical activity can help improve sleep quality, which is particularly important because poor sleep is a significant risk factor for mental health issues.

The Impact of Diet on Mental Health

Diet plays a crucial role in physical health, which in turn affects mental well-being. Nutrients dense foods support brain function and influence brain structure, potentially reducing the risk of mental health conditions. For instance:

Omega-3 Fatty Acids: Found in fish and flaxseeds, these are essential for brain health and are linked to reduced rates of depression.

B Vitamins: Vitamins such as B12 and folate have direct impacts on mood and other brain functions.

Complex Carbohydrates: These are important for maintaining consistent blood sugar levels, which can affect your mood and energy.

A balanced diet that includes a variety of foods from all food groups can promote not only physical health but also mental well-being by ensuring adequate intakes of essential nutrients.

Exercise as a Tool for Mental Wellness

Exercise is a powerful intervention that can help people recover from mental health issues and can contribute to maintaining mental well-being. Engaging in regular physical activity can have a profoundly positive impact on depression, anxiety, ADHD, and more. It also relieves stress, improves memory, helps you sleep better, and boosts your overall mood. Research indicates that modest amounts of exercise can make a difference; no matter your age or fitness level, you can learn to use exercise as a powerful tool to feel better.

Managing Chronic Conditions to Improve Mental Health

Chronic physical health conditions such as diabetes, cardiovascular disease, or obesity can increase the risk of developing mental health issues. Managing these chronic conditions with regular check-ups, medication adherence, and modifications in lifestyle can help improve mental health by reducing the burden of symptoms and improving overall quality of life.

The Benefits of Outdoor Activities

Engaging in outdoor activities like hiking, biking, or gardening can provide additional mental health benefits. Natural settings can be calming and help reduce stress, and sunlight is a major source of vitamin D, which may have protective effects against depression.

Building a Routine for Physical and Mental Health

Building a routine that incorporates elements beneficial for both physical and mental health can reinforce their interdependence and enhance overall well-being. This might include:

Regular Physical Activity: Aim for at least 150 minutes of moderate aerobic activity or 75 minutes of vigorous activity each week, along with muscle-strengthening exercises on two or more days a week.

Balanced Diet: Eat a variety of foods to ensure you get all the necessary nutrients to support physical and mental health.

Adequate Sleep: Ensure enough sleep each night to help support emotional regulation and mental health.

Mindfulness and Relaxation Techniques: Incorporate practices such as yoga, meditation, or deep breathing into your daily routine to reduce stress and improve mental focus.

Maintaining physical health is crucial for mental well-being. A holistic approach that includes diet, exercise, adequate sleep, and stress management can help enhance both physical and mental health. By understanding and leveraging the deep connection between the body and the mind, individuals can improve their overall quality of life and foster both physical and mental resilience.

"Physical health is the cornerstone of mental clarity. Take care of your body, and your mind will reward you with sharpness and peace. Every step towards health is a step towards a happier life."

THIRTEEN

Breaking Free from the Past: Letting Go and Moving Forward

Letting go of the past and moving forward is a fundamental step in achieving emotional freedom and a fulfilling life. It involves releasing negative memories, grudges, and traumas that hinder personal growth and happiness. This process is essential for anyone who seeks to embrace the present and build a positive future, but it often requires significant emotional work and introspection.

Understanding the Hold of the Past

The past can hold a powerful sway over one's life due to unresolved emotions, lingering regrets, or traumatic experiences. These memories can trigger fear, sadness, anger, or guilt, which may prevent individuals from experiencing the present fully and from envisioning a hopeful future. Understanding why the past holds such power is the first step towards letting it go. This often involves recognizing the impact of past events on one's beliefs and behaviors and acknowledging that these memories do not have to define one's identity or future.

The Psychological Impact of Past Experiences

Past experiences, especially traumatic ones, can shape a person's worldview, influence their behavior, and affect their emotional health. For example, someone who has experienced betrayal may have difficulty trusting others, or someone who has faced repeated failures may fear new challenges. These experiences can create a narrative that feels impossible to change. However, with conscious effort and support, individuals can rewrite these narratives and choose how much power their past has over their future.

Strategies for Letting Go

Acknowledge and Accept the Past: Acceptance does not mean approval but recognizing that the past occurred and cannot be changed. This acceptance is crucial in the process of letting go.

Express Your Feelings: Bottling up emotions can lead to them resurfacing in harmful ways. Finding healthy outlets for these feelings, such as therapy, journaling, or art, can facilitate healing.

Forgive: Forgiveness, whether of others or oneself, can be incredibly freeing. It involves letting go of resentment and understanding that forgiveness is more about personal peace than condoning past wrongs.

Learn from the Past: Every experience, good or bad, comes with valuable lessons. Identifying what these experiences have taught you can transform them from obstacles into stepping stones.

Create New Memories: Actively making positive experiences can help overshadow the negative memories. This might involve pursuing new interests, building new relationships, or setting new goals.

Seek Professional Help: Sometimes, professional guidance is needed to process and let go of the past, especially if it involves trauma. Therapists can provide tools and strategies tailored to individual needs.

The Role of Mindfulness in Letting Go

Mindfulness is the practice of being present and fully engaged with the current moment without judgment. This practice can be instrumental in letting go of the past because it shifts focus from past regrets or future anxieties to the here and now. Mindfulness techniques, such as meditation, deep breathing, and mindful observation, can help decrease the intensity of memories and their emotional hold.

Setting Goals for the Future

Setting goals is a powerful way to move forward. Goals give a sense of direction and purpose, which can motivate individuals to focus on the future rather than dwell on the past. These goals should be specific, measurable, achievable, relevant, and time-bound (SMART). They provide a roadmap for where you want to go and outline the steps needed to get there.

Cultivating a Supportive Network

No one has to go through the process of letting go alone. A supportive network of friends, family, or community groups can provide encouragement and understanding. Additionally, sharing experiences with others who have faced similar challenges can validate feelings and foster a sense of community and belonging.

Rebuilding Self-Identity

Letting go of the past often involves redefining one's self-identity. This may mean developing aspects of oneself that were suppressed or overlooked. Engaging in new activities, learning new skills, and meeting new people can help in forming a new self-image that reflects who you are now, not who you were in the past.

Embracing Change

Finally, embracing change as a positive and inevitable part of life can ease the process of letting go. Change allows for growth and new experiences and can be a powerful antidote to the stagnation that holding onto the past often brings.

Letting go of the past and moving forward is not just about forgetting or dismissing past experiences. It's about transforming how these experiences are viewed and how they impact current and future life. This process is about making peace with the past, embracing the present, and optimistically stepping into the future, empowered by newly gained insights and freed from the chains of past burdens.

"Letting go of the past is freeing the future. Acknowledge and learn from your history, but don't let it anchor you from moving forward. Peace comes from living in the present, not dwelling in the bygone."

♡♡♡

FOURTEEN

Deepening Connections: Relationship Building for Inner Peace

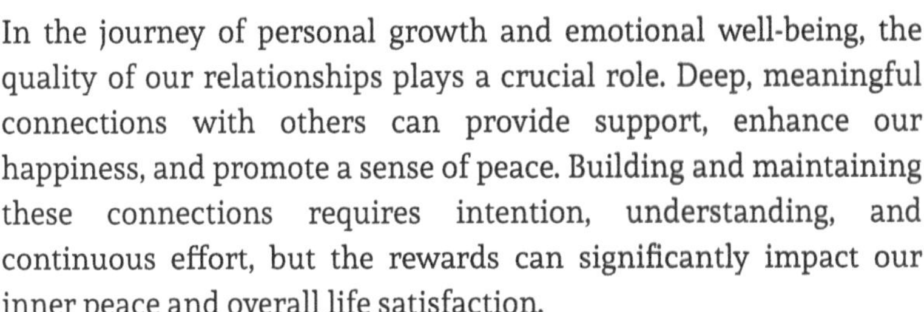

In the journey of personal growth and emotional well-being, the quality of our relationships plays a crucial role. Deep, meaningful connections with others can provide support, enhance our happiness, and promote a sense of peace. Building and maintaining these connections requires intention, understanding, and continuous effort, but the rewards can significantly impact our inner peace and overall life satisfaction.

Understanding the Importance of Relationships

Human beings are inherently social creatures, and our interactions can have profound impacts on our mental and emotional health. Positive relationships can act as buffers against stress, help us feel valued, and increase our resilience. On the other hand, strained or superficial relationships can contribute to feelings of loneliness and anxiety. Therefore, investing in our relationships not only enriches our lives but also strengthens our emotional stability and sense of fulfillment.

The Psychology Behind Connections

The foundations of strong relationships are built on trust, empathy, mutual respect, and understanding. These elements foster emotional safety, allowing individuals to express themselves freely and openly without fear of judgment. When people feel emotionally safe, they are more likely to share their thoughts and feelings, deepening the connection.

Effective Communication: The Key to Deeper Connections

Communication is the cornerstone of any relationship. Effective communication involves both expressing oneself clearly and listening actively. Here are some tips to enhance communication skills:

Active Listening: This means fully concentrating on what is being said rather than just passively hearing the words. Show your engagement by nodding, maintaining eye contact, and refraining from interrupting while the other person speaks.

Empathetic Responses: Try to understand the emotions behind the words. This involves not just hearing what the other person is saying, but also why they might be saying it, which can lead to deeper understanding and connection.

Openness and Honesty: Share your thoughts and feelings openly with others, and encourage them to do the same. This can help build trust and prevent misunderstandings that can damage relationships.

Nonverbal Cues: Pay attention to body language, tone of voice, and other nonverbal signals that can provide insight into how someone really feels.

Building Trust and Safety

Creating a sense of trust and safety is essential for deepening relationships. Trust develops over time and is reinforced by consistent behavior. You can build trust by:

Being Reliable: Do what you say you will do. Consistency in your actions allows people to feel secure in their expectations of you.

Showing Respect: Treat others with consideration and regard their feelings and thoughts as important. This includes respecting their boundaries and privacy.

Expressing Appreciation: Regularly acknowledge and appreciate the efforts and qualities of others. This positive reinforcement strengthens bonds and increases mutual respect.

Navigating Conflicts in Relationships

Conflict is a natural part of any relationship, but handling it constructively is vital for maintaining strong connections. Effective conflict resolution can actually strengthen relationships by demonstrating that challenges can be overcome. Key aspects of managing conflicts include:

Address Issues Promptly: Do not let resentments build up. Discuss issues as they arise in a calm and respectful manner.

Focus on the Problem, Not the Person: Keep discussions objective and avoid personal attacks. Discuss behaviors and situations, not inherent personal qualities.

Seek Compromise: Sometimes, agreeing to disagree is necessary. Look for solutions that satisfy both parties, recognizing that compromise is often required to resolve conflicts amicably.

Fostering Shared Experiences

Sharing experiences, whether they are challenges, adventures, or simple daily activities, can significantly deepen relationships. These shared moments create memories and can serve as the glue that binds people together. Consider activities that encourage collaboration or provide mutual enrichment, such as:

Participating in Community Services

Joining Clubs or Groups with Similar Interests

Engaging in Creative Projects Together

Prioritizing Relationships

Given the busyness of modern life, it's crucial to prioritize relationships consciously. This might mean scheduling regular time with friends and family, staying in touch through messages or calls, or simply making sure to spend quality time together during weekends or holidays.

Deepening connections and building meaningful relationships are essential for achieving inner peace and overall emotional well-being. Through effective communication, trust, and shared experiences, these connections can become sources of joy, support, and stability in our lives. Prioritizing these relationships and continuously nurturing them can lead to a richer, more fulfilling life.

♡♡♡

"Cultivating joy is like tending a garden; it requires patience, persistence, and a bit of dirt under your nails. Plant joy daily with acts of kindness, moments of connection, and laughter. Watch how it blossoms and spreads."

FIFTEEN

The Practice of Gratitude and Its Transformative Power

Gratitude is more than just saying "thank you." It's a profound practice that, when cultivated, can transform your outlook on life, enhance your well-being, and positively affect your physical and mental health. The practice of gratitude involves a conscious focus on appreciating the value of what one has and acknowledging the positive aspects of life.

Understanding Gratitude

Gratitude is an emotional response to giving and receiving; it is recognizing the good in one's life and acknowledging that some of these sources of goodness lie outside the self. This practice helps individuals connect to something larger than themselves as individuals — whether to other people, nature, or a higher power.

Psychological Benefits of Gratitude

The benefits of practicing gratitude are vast and well-documented by psychological research. Here are some of the most notable:

Enhanced Happiness: Studies have shown that gratitude can significantly increase happiness levels. By shifting focus from what is lacking or problematic to what is abundant and right, gratitude helps people appreciate their achievements and the beauty of existence.

Reduced Depression: Regular gratitude practice is associated with a decrease in symptoms of depression over time. Gratitude helps cultivate a positive mindset that can counter feelings of despair and hopelessness.

Improved Self-Esteem: Instead of becoming resentful toward others for having more (whether in terms of possessions, achievements, or qualities), grateful people are able to appreciate other people's accomplishments and contributions to their own lives.

Strengthened Relationships: Expressing gratitude can strengthen relationships. When people express gratitude towards others, it not only increases the bond but also encourages a mutual appreciation that can deepen connection and affection.

Physical Health Benefits of Gratitude

Practicing gratitude can also have tangible benefits on physical health, including:

Improved Sleep: Keeping a gratitude journal and jotting down thoughts of thankfulness before bed can help improve the quality and duration of sleep.

Better Physical Health: Grateful people are more likely to take care of their health. They exercise more often and are more likely to attend regular check-ups, which contributes to further longevity.

Reduced Stress and Enhanced Resilience: Gratitude has been linked to better coping skills during hardships and trauma. It fosters resilience by promoting a positive and hopeful attitude.

Cultivating Gratitude in Daily Life

Adopting a grateful mindset requires regular practice. Here are some strategies to help cultivate gratitude:

Keep a Gratitude Journal: Regularly write down things for which you're grateful. This could be as simple as a sunny day, a good meal, or meaningful progress on a project. The act of writing reinforces gratitude.

Gratitude Reminders: Set up visual or auditory reminders to pause and reflect on what you're grateful for. This could be a daily alarm or sticky notes placed in visible locations.

Express Gratitude to Others: Make it a habit to thank others, not just for grand gestures but for the smaller acts of kindness too. This not only enhances your own gratitude but also uplifts others.

Meditate on Gratitude: Meditation focused on gratitude involves reflecting on the gifts, benefits, and good things you enjoy. Visualization of those you are grateful for can intensify the feelings of gratitude.

Reflect During Difficult Times: Even during challenges, try to find something to be grateful for. This can shift your perspective and make the situation more manageable.

Integrating Gratitude Into Personal Values

To make gratitude a more integral part of your life, integrate it into your broader personal values and attitude towards life. Viewing life as a gift and focusing on the positives can make gratitude a more natural part of your day-to-day experiences.

The practice of gratitude is transformative, capable of bringing about significant improvements in both mental and physical health. By fostering an attitude of thankfulness and regularly practicing gratitude, individuals can enjoy enhanced well-being, stronger relationships, and a deeper appreciation for life. As gratitude becomes a habit, it can transform not just individual moments, but entire lives, leading to greater happiness and fulfillment.

"Journaling is the art of painting with words; it's where thoughts become visible, and emotions gain clarity. It's not just about recording life but understanding it. Through the pages, we discover ourselves."

SIXTEEN

SELF-DISCOVERY THROUGH JOURNALING

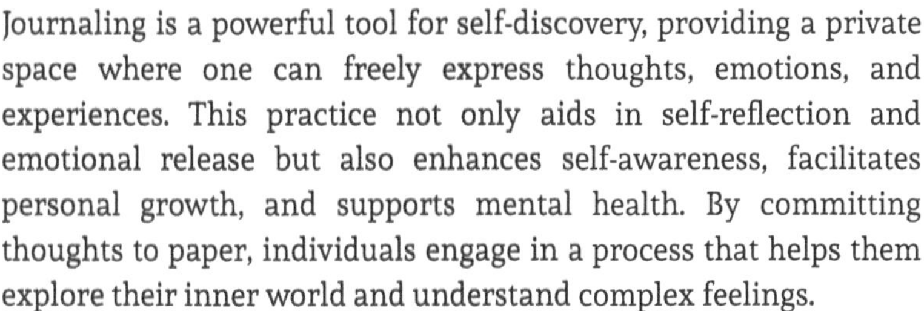

Journaling is a powerful tool for self-discovery, providing a private space where one can freely express thoughts, emotions, and experiences. This practice not only aids in self-reflection and emotional release but also enhances self-awareness, facilitates personal growth, and supports mental health. By committing thoughts to paper, individuals engage in a process that helps them explore their inner world and understand complex feelings.

The Process of Journaling

Journaling involves regularly writing down thoughts and feelings to understand them more clearly. If you struggle with stress, depression, or anxiety, keeping a journal can help you gain control of your emotions and improve your mental health. By expressing yourself on paper, you don't just release your emotions; you also engage in a process of self-exploration that can unearth new insights about yourself and the challenges you face.

Benefits of Journaling for Self-Discovery

Enhanced Self-Awareness: Journaling compels individuals to engage in introspection. This deep dive into one's thoughts and feelings can lead to greater self-awareness, providing insights into personal motivations, desires, and fears.

Emotional Release: Writing about anger, sadness, and other painful emotions helps to release the intensity of these feelings. By reading back through your journal, you can get a fresh perspective on emotional upsets, which often leads to calmer, more stable emotional states.

Stress Reduction: Journaling about stress and its sources can help clarify the stressors and reduce their impact. It's a healthy way to express what you're feeling without burdening someone else with your worries.

Problem-Solving: Unlike verbal processing, which tends to happen in a linear fashion, writing unfolds and explores patterns of behavior that contribute to complex situations. Sometimes, possible solutions emerge on the page that you might not have considered verbally.

Track Patterns and Growth: Regular entries in a journal can help track patterns in behavior and thought that are beneficial or harmful. It can also be incredibly rewarding and motivating to look back over old journals and see how much growth has occurred.

How to Start Journaling

Starting a journaling practice can seem daunting at first, but it's simpler than it sounds. Here are some tips for getting started:

Choose Your Medium: Decide whether you prefer a physical notebook or a digital journal. Each has its benefits; physical journals provide a tangible sense of progress, while digital journals are convenient and easily searchable.

Create a Routine: Set aside a regular time each day for journaling. Consistency helps develop journaling into a habit and ensures that the benefits of journaling are sustained over time.

Keep It Private: Knowing that no one else will read your journal can free you to express yourself fully without holding back, which is crucial for self-discovery.

Write Freely: Don't worry about grammar or spelling. The important thing is to get your thoughts and feelings out without censorship or revision.

Prompts to Enhance Self-Discovery

If you're unsure what to write about, here are some prompts to get you started:

What are you grateful for today?

What is a recent situation that upset you, and why?

Describe a recent dream and how it made you feel.

What are your goals for the next year, and what steps can you take towards them?

Reflect on a recent success. What did it teach you?

Journaling Techniques for Deeper Insights

Dialogue Writing: Engage in a written dialogue with different parts of yourself or even with a person or object that is not present. This can help uncover hidden feelings about relationships or personal challenges.

Stream of Consciousness: Write continuously without stopping. This technique can help bypass the conscious mind's filters, bringing subconscious thoughts and feelings to the surface.

Letter Writing: Write letters to yourself, either your past or future self. Letters can also be written to others (though not necessarily sent) to express thoughts and feelings that are difficult to communicate directly.

Integration into Daily Life

Integrating journaling into your daily life as a routine practice can transform it from a simple activity into a profound tool for personal growth and self-discovery. The more regularly you journal, the more familiar you will become with the depths of your inner self, leading to a more authentic, self-aware existence.

Journaling is a versatile and powerful tool for self-discovery. It offers a unique blend of psychological relief and self-exploration, which can foster profound personal growth and insight. As you continue to journal, you will likely find it an indispensable part of your journey towards understanding yourself and living a more conscious, fulfilled life.

"Facing your fears is the ultimate act of bravery. Each fear faced is a shadow conquered, illuminating the path to confidence. Do not shy away; every challenge overcome is a chain broken."

ღღღ

SEVENTEEN

Facing Fears: Practical Steps to Build Confidence

Fear is a powerful emotion that can either propel us forward or paralyze us. Facing our fears is not just about confronting the things that scare us, but also about building the confidence and resilience needed to handle challenges effectively. Overcoming fear involves understanding its origins, recognizing how it impacts our lives, and taking practical steps to address it head-on.

Understanding the Nature of Fear

Fear is a natural response to perceived threats. It is an essential part of human evolution, alerting us to danger and preparing us to deal with it. However, in the modern world, many of the fears we encounter are not about immediate survival but rather about social acceptance, failure, rejection, or uncertainty about the future. These fears can be more complex and require a different approach than simply "fight or flight."

The Impact of Fear on Daily Life

Unaddressed fears can limit personal and professional growth. They can manifest as anxiety, avoidance behaviors, or self-sabotage. For example, fear of failure might prevent someone from pursuing new career opportunities or returning to education. Similarly, fear of rejection could hinder someone from forming close relationships or expressing their true selves.

Practical Steps to Overcome Fear and Build Confidence

Identify Your Fears: Start by clearly identifying what you are afraid of. Write them down in detail. Understanding the specific aspects of your fear is the first step toward conquering it.

Educate Yourself: Knowledge is a powerful tool against fear. Often, fear stems from the unknown. By learning more about what frightens you, you can demystify it and reduce the fear it generates.

Gradual Exposure: Gradually expose yourself to the fear in a controlled and manageable way. This is known as desensitization and is particularly effective for phobias. For example, if you are afraid of public speaking, start by speaking to a mirror, then to a small group of friends, and gradually increase the audience size.

Cognitive Restructuring: Change the way you think about the fear. Instead of thinking, "If I fail, I will be embarrassed," think, "Everyone makes mistakes, and I can learn from mine." This shifts the focus from fearing failure to seeing it as a learning opportunity.

Build a Support Network: Having a support network can provide encouragement and make the process of facing fears less daunting. Share your goals and fears with trusted friends or family who can offer support and accountability.

Practice Mindfulness and Relaxation Techniques: Techniques such as deep breathing, meditation, or yoga can help manage the physiological responses to fear. These practices encourage a state of calmness and present-moment awareness, reducing overall anxiety.

Visualize Success: Visualization is a technique used by athletes and successful people in various fields. Regularly visualize yourself successfully facing your fears. This mental rehearsal can build confidence and reduce anxiety about actual events.

Take Care of Your Physical Health: Physical health impacts mental health significantly. Regular exercise, a healthy diet, and adequate sleep can improve your overall resilience and ability to cope with fears.

Challenge Yourself Regularly: Regularly stepping outside your comfort zone can be very effective in building confidence. Small challenges that stretch your capabilities can lead to significant growth.

Acknowledge and Celebrate Success: Recognize your progress in facing your fears, no matter how small. Celebrating victories builds confidence and reinforces the positive behavior of facing fears rather than avoiding them.

Seek Professional Help: If your fears feel overwhelming or lead to anxiety that interferes with daily life, consider seeking help from a mental health professional. Therapy can provide strategies and support to help you manage and overcome your fears.

Integrating Fear-Facing Techniques into Daily Life

Incorporating these strategies into your daily life requires commitment and persistence. It may help to keep a journal of your experiences with facing fears, noting what strategies helped and how you felt before and after the experience. Over time, these entries will not only show your progress but also help refine your approach to handling fears.

Facing fears is a dynamic process that involves understanding the nature of fear, using practical tools to manage it, and building the confidence to face not only current fears but future challenges as well. Each step taken to confront fears directly is a step toward greater personal freedom and assurance, contributing to a more engaged, fearless life.

"Creating a personal retreat is building a sanctuary for your soul. It's a place where peace is the guardian and reflection, the guide. Cherish this space, for it is where you can hear your true self most clearly."

♡♡♡

EIGHTEEN

Creating a Personal Retreat: Spaces for Solitude and Reflection

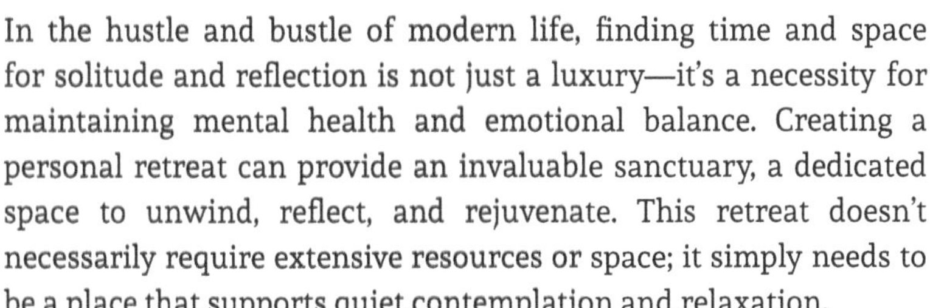
In the hustle and bustle of modern life, finding time and space for solitude and reflection is not just a luxury—it's a necessity for maintaining mental health and emotional balance. Creating a personal retreat can provide an invaluable sanctuary, a dedicated space to unwind, reflect, and rejuvenate. This retreat doesn't necessarily require extensive resources or space; it simply needs to be a place that supports quiet contemplation and relaxation.

The Importance of Solitude and Reflection

Solitude and reflection offer numerous benefits, including improved concentration, increased self-awareness, and deeper relaxation. In solitude, one can step back from the pressures of daily life, gain perspective on ongoing challenges, and reconnect with inner desires and motivations. This practice allows for a reset of the mind and emotions, leading to enhanced creativity and problem-solving skills.

Choosing the Right Space

The first step in creating a personal retreat is selecting an appropriate space. This could be a small room in your home, a garden, a quiet corner with a comfortable chair, or even a dedicated nook that can be personalized. The key is to find a space that feels safe and separate from the daily flow of life at home or work.

Designing Your Retreat

Once you have identified the space, the next step is to design it to encourage relaxation and reflection. Here are some elements to consider:

Comfort: Include comfortable seating like a plush chair or a soft rug with cushions. The physical comfort provided by these elements can help ease the mind into a state of relaxation.

Simplicity: Keep the decor simple and uncluttered. A minimalist approach can help clear the mind of distractions and promote calmness.

Nature: Incorporating elements of nature, such as plants, water features, or simply a vase of fresh flowers, can enhance the sense of tranquility in your space.

Light: Natural light is ideal for a retreat space. If possible, choose a location with good natural light. Alternatively, use soft and warm artificial lighting to create a soothing atmosphere.

Personal Touches: Add personal items that inspire relaxation and reflection, such as books, art, or items from nature. These should be things that bring you joy and peace.

Sound: Consider the auditory environment of your retreat. Soft background music, nature sounds, or simply a quiet space can be profoundly calming.

Scent: Aromatherapy can significantly affect mood. Essential oils like lavender, sandalwood, or cedarwood can be calming and grounding.

Establishing a Routine

Creating the space is only part of the process; the real benefit comes from regular use. Establishing a routine that incorporates time spent in your personal retreat can help solidify its value in your life. Even just a few minutes a day spent in meditation, journaling, or simply sitting quietly can make a significant difference in your overall well-being.

Activities for Your Personal Retreat

The activities you choose to engage in during your retreat time should reflect your personal needs and what you find most restorative. Here are a few suggestions:

Meditation and Breathing Exercises: These practices can help reduce stress, enhance concentration, and promote a deeper sense of peace.

Reading and Writing: Engage in reflective writing, such as journaling or creative writing. Reading can also be a great way to relax and expand your thoughts.

Artistic Activities: Drawing, painting, or crafting can be therapeutic ways to express oneself and decompress.

Yoga or Gentle Stretching: These physical activities can help relieve tension and focus the mind.

Mindful Observation: Spend time simply observing the details of your surroundings or your personal sensory experiences. This can help anchor you in the present moment.

Maintaining and Evolving Your Space

As you grow and change, your needs for your retreat might also evolve. Periodically reassess your space and how you use it. Updating your retreat to reflect your current mental and emotional state ensures that it remains a relevant and supportive resource.

Creating a personal retreat is about carving out a physical and psychological space for solitude and reflection. This space, whether simple or elaborate, acts as a sanctuary from the stresses of daily life and provides a venue for personal growth and emotional reset. Regular use of this space can foster significant improvements in mental health, creativity, and overall life satisfaction, making it a wise investment in your well-being.

"Joy is contagious; the more you share, the more it grows. Find what makes your heart sing and create moments to celebrate it. Joy nurtured in solitude blooms in the company."

NINETEEN

Cultivating Joy: Activities that Lift the Spirit

In the pursuit of a fulfilled and balanced life, cultivating joy is essential. Joy is more than fleeting happiness; it is a deeper, more sustained feeling that can significantly enhance quality of life and improve overall well-being. Engaging in activities that lift the spirit is not just about experiencing moments of happiness, but about nurturing a lasting state of joy that can support one through all facets of life.

Understanding the Nature of Joy

Joy is an emotion that transcends mere happiness by embedding a sense of deep satisfaction and contentment. It arises from engaging in activities that are meaningful, fulfilling, and pleasurable. Unlike happiness, which can be influenced by external circumstances, joy is often derived from internal fulfillment and peace.

Activities to Cultivate Joy

The activities that can foster joy vary widely depending on individual preferences, values, and lifestyles. However, some universal activities have been shown to boost joy consistently across different people. Here are some practical ways to cultivate joy in everyday life:

Connecting with Nature: Spending time in natural settings can have a profound effect on your mood. Activities like hiking, gardening, or simply taking a walk in a local park can help you feel more peaceful and grounded, enhancing your overall sense of joy.

Creative Expression: Engaging in creative activities such as painting, writing, music, or dance allows for self-expression and can be incredibly fulfilling. Creativity not only stimulates the mind but also provides a sense of accomplishment and joy.

Mindful Practices: Practices like yoga, meditation, and tai chi not only reduce stress but also enhance mindfulness and presence, which are closely linked to joy. By focusing on the present moment and appreciating life as it is, one can cultivate a deeper sense of joy.

Physical Activity: Exercise releases endorphins, chemicals in your brain that act as natural mood lifters. Regular physical activity can elevate your mood and energy levels, enhancing your overall sense of joy.

Volunteering and Helping Others: Altruistic behaviors have a significant impact on emotional well-being. Helping others can provide a sense of purpose and fulfillment that is deeply joyful.

Social Connections: Building and maintaining positive relationships with friends and family is crucial for emotional health. Strong social support systems lead to shared joys and reduced stress, contributing to overall happiness and contentment.

Cultivating Gratitude: Keeping a gratitude journal or simply taking time daily to reflect on what you are thankful for can shift your focus from what is lacking to what is abundant in your life, fostering a sense of joy.

Learning and Curiosity: Pursuing new knowledge and skills can be incredibly rewarding. Whether it's learning a new language, picking up a new hobby, or exploring new places, the excitement of discovery can bring joy and invigorate your life.

Routine Detox and Unplugging: Regularly taking time away from electronic devices and hectic schedules can help reset your mental state. Periods of unplugging allow you to reconnect with yourself and your environment, often leading to a renewed sense of joy.

Listening to Music: Music has the power to uplift and inspire. Listening to your favorite music, or exploring new genres, can enhance your mood and provide an instant boost to your spirit.

Integrating Joyful Activities into Everyday Life

To successfully integrate these activities into your life, consider the following strategies:

Set Joyful Intentions: Start each day by setting an intention to engage in at least one activity that brings you joy. This can help make joy a regular part of your life rather than something that happens sporadically.

Plan for Joy: Just as you might schedule meetings or appointments, schedule time for activities that bring you joy. This ensures that these activities are a priority and not overlooked in the busyness of daily life.

Reflect on Joy: Spend some time each week reflecting on what activities brought you the most joy and why. This reflection can help you understand what brings you the most fulfillment and how you can incorporate more of it into your life.

Be Open to New Experiences: Sometimes, joy comes from unexpected sources. Be open to trying new activities or revisiting past interests that you may have set aside.

Cultivating joy involves more than just engaging in enjoyable activities; it requires a conscious effort to incorporate these activities into everyday life. By understanding what brings you joy and making a deliberate effort to seek out and engage in these activities, you can enhance your overall well-being and lead a more fulfilled and contented life.

"Reflecting on your journey is essential; it allows you to see not just where you've been, but how far you've come. Reflection turns experience into insight and mistakes into wisdom. Always look back with an eye to move forward."

TWENTY

Reflections and Road Ahead: Maintaining Confidence and Peace

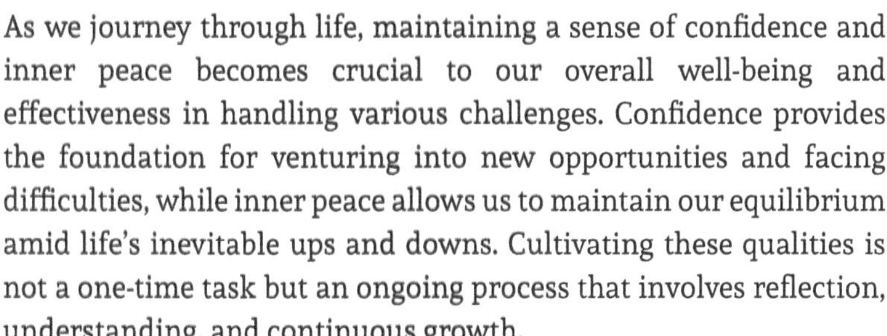

As we journey through life, maintaining a sense of confidence and inner peace becomes crucial to our overall well-being and effectiveness in handling various challenges. Confidence provides the foundation for venturing into new opportunities and facing difficulties, while inner peace allows us to maintain our equilibrium amid life's inevitable ups and downs. Cultivating these qualities is not a one-time task but an ongoing process that involves reflection, understanding, and continuous growth.

Understanding Confidence and Inner Peace

Confidence is not just about feeling assured in one's abilities but also about possessing a quiet understanding that one can handle the situation at hand, regardless of the outcome. It's about trust in one's capabilities and decisions. Inner peace, on the other hand, is the state of being mentally and spiritually at ease, with enough knowledge and understanding to keep oneself strong in the face of discord or stress.

Reflecting on Past Experiences

One of the key strategies for maintaining confidence and peace is to reflect on past experiences. Reflection allows us to consider what we've learned from our successes and failures. It involves looking back at situations where we felt particularly confident or peaceful and understanding what contributed to those feelings. Similarly, reflecting on less positive experiences can help identify what might have shaken our confidence or disturbed our peace, providing clues on how to handle similar situations better in the future.

Setting Realistic Goals

Setting realistic goals plays a significant role in maintaining confidence and inner peace. Goals give us direction and a sense of purpose, making it easier to navigate through life. When setting goals, it's important to ensure they are achievable and aligned with our values and capabilities. This alignment helps prevent the feelings of frustration and failure that come from setting unrealistic expectations.

Developing Resilience

Resilience is the ability to bounce back from setbacks and failures, and it is crucial for maintaining confidence. Developing resilience can involve several strategies, including:

Embracing Failure as a Learning Opportunity: Instead of seeing failure as a negative endpoint, view it as a chance to learn and grow, which can help maintain confidence and readiness to face future challenges.

Maintaining a Support Network: Having a reliable support network can provide encouragement and perspective when you're feeling down or overwhelmed.

Staying Flexible: Being adaptable in the face of change or obstacles can help sustain your inner peace and confidence, as you're less likely to feel thrown off by unexpected events.

Practicing Mindfulness and Meditation

Mindfulness and meditation are powerful tools for maintaining inner peace. They involve focusing on the present moment and accepting it without judgment. Regular practice can help reduce stress, enhance emotional health, and improve overall well-being, which are crucial for maintaining peace and confidence.

Nurturing Positive Relationships

The quality of our relationships significantly affects our mental and emotional health. Nurturing positive relationships can provide emotional support and increase our sense of connectedness and security, enhancing both peace and confidence.

Maintaining Physical Health

Physical health has a direct impact on mental and emotional well-being. Regular physical activity, a balanced diet, and adequate sleep can improve mood and energy levels, thereby supporting both confidence and inner peace.

Continuous Learning and Growth

Adopting a mindset of continuous learning and personal growth can help maintain confidence. This involves being open to new experiences and willing to acquire new knowledge and skills. Continuous growth fosters a sense of progression, which can be incredibly empowering.

Preparing for the Road Ahead

Looking forward, it's important to anticipate potential challenges and prepare for them. This preparation can involve strategic planning, seeking advice or mentorship, and continuing to develop skills that will be useful in future situations.

Embracing Change

Finally, maintaining confidence and peace requires an acceptance of change. Change is inevitable, and embracing it can reduce anxiety and resistance, making it easier to maintain peace and adapt confidently to new circumstances.

Maintaining confidence and inner peace is an ongoing process that involves reflection, understanding oneself, and actively engaging in practices that support mental, emotional, and physical health. By setting realistic goals, developing resilience, nurturing positive relationships, and embracing continuous learning and change, one can ensure they are well-equipped to handle the future with confidence and maintain a serene state of mind.

"Maintaining peace and confidence doesn't happen by chance; it's a deliberate choice, a daily practice. Cultivate these qualities like precious plants in your garden of well-being. Water them with mindfulness, and feed them with gratitude."

♡♡♡

TWENTY-ONE
SUMMARY

Embarking on the journey of this book invites readers into a profound exploration of self-trust and the development of a serene, confident life. This book intertwines psychological wisdom, actionable guidance, and personal insight, offering a comprehensive guide to not just coping with life's challenges, but thriving amidst them.

Embracing Vulnerability as a Strength

The first step in trusting oneself is embracing vulnerability. Vulnerability is not a sign of weakness but a courageous acknowledgment of one's true self. It requires openness to experiences and accepting oneself, including one's fears and flaws. By embracing vulnerability, we allow ourselves to experience growth and transformation, fostering a deep sense of trust in our abilities and decisions.

Understanding and Overcoming Anxiety

Anxiety can often feel like a barrier to self-trust. By understanding its roots and manifestations, we can develop strategies to manage and alleviate it. Techniques such as mindfulness, cognitive-behavioral approaches, and lifestyle changes play crucial roles in transforming anxiety from an overwhelming force to a manageable aspect of life, thus restoring peace and confidence.

Harnessing the Power of Positive Self-Talk

Positive self-talk is vital for building self-esteem and overcoming negative thought patterns. It involves consciously replacing critical or negative thoughts with affirming and constructive ones. This shift not only enhances self-trust but also actively contributes to a more optimistic outlook on life, fostering deeper resilience against challenges.

The Healing Power of Mindfulness

Mindfulness meditation offers a tool for remaining anchored in the present moment, reducing stress and promoting a state of calm. By practicing mindfulness, we can better manage our emotional responses and maintain a clear perspective, which is crucial for both facing immediate challenges and planning for long-term goals.

Decoding and Managing Stress

Understanding the sources and effects of stress is essential for maintaining mental balance and physical health. By adopting stress reduction techniques such as relaxation exercises, time management, and setting realistic goals, individuals can enhance their resilience, reduce anxiety, and cultivate a more peaceful life.

Building and Reclaiming Resilience

Resilience is the ability to bounce back from setbacks and adapt to adversity without losing one's core integrity. Building resilience involves understanding past failures and successes, setting realistic expectations, and maintaining a positive, yet realistic outlook. Resilience does not eliminate stress or erase life's difficulties, but it does equip individuals with the tools to handle them effectively and maintain inner peace.

Visualizing Success and Inner Peace

Visualization techniques are powerful tools for personal transformation. They involve envisioning positive outcomes and experiences, which can enhance motivation and clarify the steps needed to achieve personal goals. Regular practice of visualization can strengthen mental resilience and support the journey toward self-trust and peace.

Cultivating Emotional Intelligence

Developing emotional intelligence is crucial for understanding and managing one's emotions, as well as fostering strong interpersonal relationships. This skill set, encompassing self-awareness, empathy, and regulation of emotions, is fundamental for personal and professional success, contributing significantly to a peaceful and confident life.

Setting Boundaries for a Balanced Life

Learning to set healthy boundaries is essential for personal well-being and effective relationship management. Boundaries help define what we are comfortable with and how we wish to be treated by others. They are vital for mutual respect and support in any relationship and contribute to a healthy, balanced lifestyle.

Achieving Work-Life Balance

Maintaining a balance between professional responsibilities and personal life is crucial for long-term happiness and stress management. Effective strategies include prioritizing tasks, delegating, and setting aside time for personal interests and relaxation. Achieving this balance is key to sustaining both career success and personal happiness.

Harnessing Intuition

Listening to and trusting one's intuition involves recognizing and valuing the inner voice that guides decisions. Intuition is a powerful cognitive process that, when honed, can significantly enhance decision-making capabilities and increase self-trust.

The Role of Physical Health in Mental Well-being

Physical health directly impacts mental well-being. Regular physical activity, a balanced diet, and sufficient sleep are foundational to maintaining both physical and mental health. These elements are interconnected; neglecting one can adversely affect the other, highlighting the need for a holistic approach to health.

Letting Go of the Past

Moving forward in life often requires letting go of past burdens and grievances. This chapter explores practical steps for releasing past hurts through forgiveness, acceptance, and focusing on the present. It's a vital process for those seeking to live a life unencumbered by past difficulties.

Fostering Joy and Gratitude

Activities that promote joy and an attitude of gratitude significantly enhance life's quality. Whether through creative expression, physical activity, or mindfulness practices, finding daily sources of joy and regularly practicing gratitude can transform one's outlook on life.

Journaling for Self-Discovery

Journaling is a powerful self-help tool that promotes self-awareness and emotional clarity. It serves as a reflective practice that can unearth deep insights about personal values, desires, and thoughts, aiding in the journey of self-discovery and personal growth.

Facing and Overcoming Fears

Confronting fears is not just about reducing anxiety but about expanding personal boundaries and enhancing self-confidence. This book discusses strategies for facing fears head-on, using tools such as systematic desensitization, cognitive restructuring, and the support of a nurturing community.

Creating Spaces for Reflection

Designing personal retreats facilitates solitude and introspection, which are essential for continuous personal growth. These spaces provide a sanctuary where one can reflect on personal goals, relax, and cultivate a deeper sense of self.

Maintaining Confidence and Peace

Looking forward, maintaining confidence and inner peace requires continuous effort. This involves adapting to life's changes, embracing new challenges, and consistently applying the principles of self-trust and peace cultivated throughout this book.

Citation And References

This book represents the culmination of extensive research and meticulous analysis, incorporating a diverse range of sources, including numerous books, scholarly studies, and personal experiences. Additionally, I have scoured various websites to gather relevant information and data essential for the compilation of this work. I have taken every precaution to ensure the accuracy of the information presented and have diligently cited all sources to acknowledge their contributions.

Despite these efforts, the possibility of inadvertent errors remains. I deeply value the insights of my readers and appreciate any feedback that can help identify and rectify such inaccuracies. I encourage you to bring any discrepancies to my attention.

Your feedback is not only welcome but crucial, as it will aid in correcting current editions and enhancing the content of future ones. I am committed to maintaining the highest standards of accuracy and reliability in my work and thank you for your support and understanding.

Additionally, I firmly uphold the principle of freedom of speech and expression as guaranteed under Article 19(1)(a) of the Constitution of India, and I respect the diverse viewpoints and expressions of all readers.

Other Books Of The Author

1. Empowering Minds: A Journey into Women's Self-Discovery and Power
2. The Dynamics of Motivation: Catalyzing Thought into Action
3. Meditation and Mental Well Being: The Path to Inner Peace and Clarity
4. The Psychology of Child Education: Nurturing Future Generations
5. Ethical Enlightenment: A Modern Guide to Living with Integrity
6. Voices of Empowerment: Stories of Women Rising Against Odds
7. Social Psychology in Everyday Life: Understanding Human Connections
8. The Essence of Motivational Speaking: Inspiring Change in Others
9. Balancing Acts: Women, Work, and the Will to Lead
10. Guiding with Grace: Raising Children with Compassion and Awareness
11. The Power of Positive Aging: Embracing Life After Fifty
12. Building Resilient Communities: Social Work in Action
13. The Ethical Educator: Principles for Teaching and Learning
14. From Insight to Impact: Social Psychology for a Better World
15. The Ethics of Empathy: A Guide to Ethical Living
16. The Science of Empowering the Self: Navigating Life's Challenges with Psychological Wisdom
17. The Mindful Conscious Leader: Meditation Techniques for Modern Management
18. Pioneering Spirit: Women's Pathways to Leadership and Empowerment
19. Feeling to Healing: The Role of Emotional Intelligence in Child Development
20. Transformative Talks and Words of Inspiration: Insights into Motivational Oratory

21. The Hidden Path to Ethical Sustainability: Crafting a Greener Tomorrow
22. Spiritual Integrity: Navigating Life with Moral Compassion
23. Clean Living, Clean Society: The Ethics of Cleanliness
24. Patriotic Spirits: Building a Nation on Positive Attitudes
25. Innovative Integrity & Vibrant Visions: The Ethical and Entrepreneurial Spirit of Gujarat
26. Youthful Visions, Endless Possibilities: Inspiring Ethics and Motivation in Children
27. Living Your Legacy: How to Motivate Others by Living Your Values
28. Secret of Healing Conversations: Ethical Practices in Counselling and Therapy
29. Creative Kindness: Crafting a Life of Compassion and Creativity
30. The Power of Appreciation: How Gratitude Can Transform Your Relationships
31. Bhagavad-Gita: Messages
32. Science of Art: The New Frontier of Fashion Modernism
33. Vivekananda's Virtues: A Blueprint for Modern Living
34. Empower Her: Navigating the Path to Women's Entrepreneurship
35. The Boundless Classroom: Innovations in Global Education
36. The Language of Leadership: Communicating with Authenticity and Impact
37. The Warrior's Mantra: Deciphering the Hanuman Chalisa
38. Echoes of Empathy: Transformative Stories of Social Service
39. Artful Living: Cultivating Creativity in Your Daily Routine
40. Finding Your Why: Discovering Your Passions and Charting Your Course
41. The Role of Social Media in Shaping Self-Esteem and Interpersonal Relationships among Adolescents

Dr. Minakshi Bansal
Social Activist
Ahmedabad, Gujarat, Bharat
minakshiindiag20@yahoo.com

|| LOKAHA SAMASTHAHA SUKHINO BHAVANTU ||

www.ingramcontent.com/pod-product-compliance
Lightning Source LLC
Chambersburg PA
CBHW030859120726
48008CB00002B/48
9798894150789